Mind
CAPTURES

Mind CAPTURES

A Man's Search to Bring Meaning to His Life and the Lives of Others by Writing Ninety-Nine Poems, Short Stories, and Essays

MICHAEL KING

MIND CAPTURES
A MAN'S SEARCH TO BRING MEANING TO HIS LIFE AND THE LIVES OF OTHERS BY WRITING NINETY-NINE POEMS, SHORT STORIES, AND ESSAYS

Copyright © 2016 Michael King.

All rights reserved. No part of this book may be used or reproduced by any means, graphic, electronic, or mechanical, including photocopying, recording, taping or by any information storage retrieval system without the written permission of the author except in the case of brief quotations embodied in critical articles and reviews.

iUniverse books may be ordered through booksellers or by contacting:

iUniverse
1663 Liberty Drive
Bloomington, IN 47403
www.iuniverse.com
1-800-Authors (1-800-288-4677)

Because of the dynamic nature of the Internet, any web addresses or links contained in this book may have changed since publication and may no longer be valid. The views expressed in this work are solely those of the author and do not necessarily reflect the views of the publisher, and the publisher hereby disclaims any responsibility for them.

Any people depicted in stock imagery provided by Thinkstock are models, and such images are being used for illustrative purposes only. Certain stock imagery © Thinkstock.

ISBN: 978-1-4917-9784-6 (sc)
ISBN: 978-1-4917-9786-0 (hc)
ISBN: 978-1-4917-9785-3 (e)

Library of Congress Control Number: 2016908428

Print information available on the last page.

iUniverse rev. date: 07/22/2016

Contents

Preface xi

1. Metastasis 1
2. All the President's Men 3
3. Pester and Resolve 5
4. Fours 8
5. Right to Strife 10
6. Ecstasy 12
7. Thirty-One 13
8. Tornado of Fire 14
9. Distant Remembrance for a New Future 15
10. Le Cou 17
11. Lamentation 18
12. Visitation 19
13. Tight-Mouthed Life 23
14. Every Time 25
15. Entwined in Rhythm 26
16. Melancholy 27
17. Frack 29
18. Li'l One 31
19. Awaken 32
20. Place of Rest 33
21. Battlefield of My Mind 35
22. Outcome 39
23. Stretch and Withstand 40
24. Small Miracles 42
25. Twenty Inspired Souls 43
26. Helpless Hand 44
27. Fountain of Proof 45
28. The Power of Words 46
29. Praiseworthy Praise Worthless 47

30. Six 49
31. Homer 50
32. Hard Air 51
33. All over the Map 52
34. Changed State 53
35. Time to Grow 54
36. Lotion for the Soul 55
37. Horizon 56
38. Change Point 57
39. Four by Twelve 58
40. Chris and Luke 60
41. Momentary Retirement 62
42. Ruminations of a Successful Woman 63
43. To the Moon 65
44. Nourishment in Three Parts 66
45. Chlorophyll Fading 67
46. A New Hope 68
47. The Clearing 70
48. Cartographer's Heart 71
49. Tidal Joys 73
50. Clean Sweep 74
51. Specific Contractor 78
52. Return to Sender—Are You Kidding Me? 79
53. Sleepy-Time Bus 80
54. Jilted Winner 81
55. Dreamscape 82
56. Admiral and the Crew 83
57. Royal "Oui" 84
58. Halftime 85
59. And the Creator Answered … 86
60. In a Small Package Is Greatness 87
61. Fourteen Lines—Are You Tracking? 88
62. One Time … Once More 89
63. Escape 90
64. Lovesick 91
65. Attachment and Release 92
66. So Many Variables 93

67. Recover	95
68. Choke Hold	96
69. See Multiple Shades	97
70. Rut in My Gut	98
71. E-Mythology	99
72. Right Number	100
73. Oh My …	101
74. SMV Number 3	102
75. Do Not Disturb	103
76. Again	105
77. Detroit	107
78. Mocked	109
79. Six Things	110
80. Agent Orange	112
81. Art History	114
82. Four More Years?	115
83. Kisses	117
84. CALaMity	118
85. Les Yeux	119
86. Revolving Door	120
87. Love Control	121
88. Steel-Toed Boots Required	122
89. Illuminated Lover	123
90. Red Dress	125
91. You Have Been Served	127
92. Crevices	129
93. Alone and Loving It	130
94. Order of the Genie	131
95. Clear Thought in a Moment of Hope	133
96. The Protector	134
97. Carrying Costs	136
98. Sleeping Cranes	137
99. I Have Found My Way Home	138
What Is Your Poem and Story to Tell?	139

This effort is dedicated to Karen K. and Dianna K. These two women have greatly influenced my life and impacted my growth trajectory. I am grateful to them both and love them for being the mirror and light in my existense.

I would also like to thank Paul B., Annie B. and Reed M. for inviting me into their lives, watering my dreams, and allowing me to grow into the person that became able to write this book.

PREFACE

Thank you for purchasing, reading, lending, and/or giving (to yourself or to others) this book. I wrote this collection of poems, stories, and essays to inspire creativity and passion in you, in whatever you are doing in your life at the moment or in the near future.

This book is about the little moments that spring up while you're engaging in life—those moments that can happen at any time. I find they almost sneak up on me as I am going about my daily business. This book contains words and comments I have heard over time. Listening to them inspired me to write a phrase, a poem, or a short story, for myself and for you. Some pieces are short; some are longer. Some I wrote down immediately; others I extracted from the past. All these experiences are part of this book that has become a part of me. I hope it will in some way become a part of you too.

This book was initially intended to be about leadership, containing poetry and short stories, but I soon realized that it was about more than just leadership. It is about those life lessons discovered along the way as you go about some primary task in the moment. Standing in the line at a coffeehouse and hearing an amusing story that makes you smile and wonder what you would do in that situation. Getting off the phone with clients and knowing that they are ignoring your advice to their own detriment. You wish you could tell them in an unfiltered manner what is really going to happen, and yet you refrain from doing so. Your clients have made it crystal clear that you are the executor of their wishes, not their trusted advisor who is tied to their best interests. Another example might be watching your little ones do something that is sure to bring falls, screams, and tears. You're unable to protect them from falling because, before you can get the first word out of your mouth, the deed has been done. And all you can do now is to be there to console and love them. In short, these moments are the little gems of life that come to you and teach you how to be more thoughtful as you go about your day. That is what I endeavored to capture in the poems, short stories, and essays in this book. Daydreaming, being inefficient, and taking time out to ponder what should be written, in an almost monk-like pursuit to write this book, fueled my desire to ultimately complete this collection.

This book is for me as much as it is for you. I desired to provide options for you to consider as you navigate this world and choose ways to contribute your important and needed talents. May this book grow with you as you grow, and may you always grow in elegance, wisdom, and strength. Maybe a phrase or poem within this book will be an encouragement to you, and if that is the case, then I am grateful for this opportunity to connect these words to you in a way that might not have ever happened if I had not written this book.

Have fun, live fully, and love passionately, because the world needs you more than ever before. Make love to life today and every day.

Blessings to you.

—Michael King

Metastasis

What is this cancer that wrecks my body?

It is as real as my heart. I can't see it, yet I know it is there.
It is a sickness in my head.
It will not exit or be forced out of its cellular prison.
It is a life sentence without parole. Who needs parole when a thirty-year sentence is cut short by a disease that will render me dead more quickly than a lethal injection could and that is more effective than Juliet's poison or Romeo's dagger?

Slipping.
Gripping.
Diving.
Delivering.

Slipping from my grasp is my destiny. I rebel; I fight more fiercely than an Apache warrior.

Gripping my life tightly, I choose to fight first and give up later.

Diving into the Internet, I gain knowledge to help heal myself.

Delivering on my promise to myself, I relish each individual victory, knowing that the war will eventually be won by death.

Cancer cares nothing for me. Cancer only cares to ensure that I can pay the extortionists the ransom demanded for drugs that embalm me like a science-class specimen soaked in formaldehyde.

It seeks to control my physical demise, like an auto-kill switch that increases its speed with every breath I take.

So I will not give in or bend to your ravishment of my mental health and my physical body.

I will move, inhale, exhale, exult, and proclaim until my last breath has been forced from my lips.

To give, love, and win as if today is my last.

For I know not when heaven's horn will be blown to call me home.

Rest.

All the President's Men

What does money mean to me?

Money makes my heart ache like the heart of a boy who yearns for the comfort of his father after he is injured at play. Money makes my freedom inevitable, like an exonerated man who served time for a white-collar crime he did not commit.

Money, your loveliness never fails to give up on me. Money, you never run out on me in the night. Money, it's your love for me that comforts me.

You make me dream and dream again because your reward is so real for me. You take what goes on in my head and create a real purpose in my life that I can trade for the things I would have to live in, live on, and live with.

My heart is on a craggy rock's edge, and I do not want to feel vulnerable for lack of money.

So I choose to raise my arms to God and allow my love to flow upward to you. Your light flows down to me and through me so that I don't crash my life at the rocky base of the mountain peak.

And I will gladly let George, Thomas, Abraham, Alexander, Andrew, Ulysses, Benjamin, William, Grover, Salmon, James, and even Woodrow come to me as my lovers in life.

In so doing, I will no longer allow my responsibility to my lovers to falter; nor will I take their love for granted.

For they have all come to me in their own special way to give me all the encouragement that I need, as a lover very well should.

Thank you for loving and respecting me, and I will in kind love and respect all those you give to me in return.

Pester and Resolve

Hope,

why do you seem so indestructible?

I have banished you from my presence, from my sight, and from my mind, and yet you take root inside me, like a weed in the crack of the sidewalk.

Protected by concrete on all sides, I cannot get my shovel between the cracks to gouge you out by the root.

In anger and frustration, I pull out all your blades of growth, but because I can't get to your roots, you always come back.

I know this is an act of futility, and I still do it anyway. I just can't stand the sight of your resiliency, because you always come back no matter what.

The most powerful poison would do no good, for if I could kill you now, then two more of you would show up in that very same crack.

If I were to seal the crack, you would patiently find a new crack and then take root there.

Is there nothing I can do to be rid of you?

You mar my concrete landscape and create chaos in my desolate world.

Must you remind me that there is an area where mediocrity cannot be cemented permanently in place?

So after a lifetime of striving to keep you out, I have decided to just give up and let you grow.

I will no longer waste energy on your removal, for clearly you endeavor to exist and expand.

Are you so brazen as to think that you can overturn concrete?

If I let you, you would consume the flat and even surface of my mortared life, and life as I know it not would become life as I know it, cracked open by your efforts to grow.

You spring forth from a minuscule seed so small that a breeze can take you away; in time, you would become nothing, dashed against the rocks or left to drown in the sea.

And yet, miraculously, as if by design, you still would have taken root in that weak place of my landscape and forever rendered my world a war zone.

You exist in that space between okay and exceptional.

You remind me that only one seed is necessary to bring about an explosion of verdant growth.

So now I'll take you for granted, and I'll expect you to become ever greater, ever stronger, ever more tenacious, until there is no room left for the hard surfaces of mediocrity in me.

Grow forth and proliferate, for I have grown weary against your desires. I will get out of your way and allow you to create a new way for me to grow way beyond what I could have ever imagined or expected from a mere crack in my landscape.

Hope,

you do seem so relentless, so endless, and so energetic.

I do like that about you in my landscape as the sun rises over the view shed of my life.

Fours

Take a moment.
Take an hour.
Take a week.
Take a nap.

Allow your mind to have some time to rest and create a new idea.

Take a day.
Take a month.
Take a year.
Take a seat.

And let your foes spend every moment working toward their own defeat.

Take a minute.
Take half a day.
Take two weeks.
Take a suite

of hotel rooms for yourself, and know it's money well spent on a good retreat.

What makes you think for all your toils and all your tasking and all your efforts that a brilliant idea shall come forth from all your incessant chatter chasing?

What makes you think a hot shower before a rest is a wasteful time at best—or a somber book all day will cause your return on investment to decay?

As your meaningful managers mentor and miss the soft tenor of the cantor, a song or a breeze carrying tomorrow's or next year's pleasing assistance to the many, do you dare take a chance with any of your time to let expand an idea whose time will come if you would just

slow down,
stop,
listen,
and listen some more

before you act.

Right to Strife

Are you pro-obstruction or anti-obstruction?

I never know exactly how to answer this question, since it is an impossibly gray area to think about and respond to in either the affirmative or the negative.

As a man who believes in God, I would love to join the ranks of my fellow countrymen and say, "Yes, I am against abortion."

I also know that women of color are more likely to experience social inequity and engage in careers that would have them choose an alternative path to well-being and need to avoid unwanted pregnancy. From that context, I would therefore find this option beyond my jurisdiction.

As a man who has never had children but wanted them, I lament the idea that anyone would actually want to terminate a pregnancy, for I could never do that to a child I was responsible for creating.

How could I actually answer affirmatively to this question?

I could answer yes to this question when men can have access to free sterilizations if they choose it. Women couldn't get pregnant if men didn't impregnate them.

I could answer yes to this question if women had access to free vocational and collegiate education to improve their opportunities to access careers that challenge them, providing alternative means of self-expression and enjoyment for them so that they wouldn't consider sex their only option, especially when that choice is not the best option for them.

I could answer yes when those who believe in God (more commonly known as the church) put more energy and attention into placing orphaned and unwanted children into families where they could grow and bring peace and healing to our country. I believe this one action is the most important thing that the church—and society—can do to render itself more just and civil in the future.

I really hate the fact that I feel both guilty about being anti-obstruction in principle and pro-obstruction in principle as well.

Has there ever been a society in history that has fully valued the contributions of women, without denigrating women in some way as well?

Can this idea of a world or nation without abortion truly exist from a lack of desire rather than from an obstruction to access?

What could or would my contribution to that reality be?

Now these are the questions I would really like to find and implement answers to.

Ecstasy

Whizzing,
Whirring,
Imagination blurring.

Past the point of no return, don't crash and burn.

Downhill skiing,
The exhilaration of speeding;
It's legal frozen liquid, a junkie's paradise through powdery turns.

Shaking steadily,
A breath that's heavenly,
A mountain of cocaine powder to cut and to kill.

The thrill of the wind noise,
A pinnacle of exploits,
That never delivers the same path twice.

Nice.

Thirty-One

From all things possible
and all things probable,
I am
the one who knows
her desire to please and deliver.

If love were a shape,
what form would it take?
A cube?

What does being
a good listener sound like in training?

Name your number of years
as the number of your marriage.
Does thirty-one seem enough?
If you knew that in advance, what would you do?

Tornado of Fire

Passion.
It is the engine that keeps a dream moving when the engine of discipline desires to stall out and quit.

Time.
Pressure.
Intensity.
Fear.
Exhilaration.
Patience.
Anger.
Joy.
Immense joy.
Opportunity.

Repetition, repetition, repetition.

Bake at 350 degrees, for a decade.
A recipe to make the most challenged of entrepreneurs a happy person.

Distant Remembrance for a New Future

Eighty years ago, you were a twinkle in the mind's eye of a certain martyr, not knowing of the invasions to come.

A seed, a new star, a young shoot; any such metaphor can explain aptly a new beginning.

However, your legacy will determine which words can explain my end.

Things can start and end on a definite date, so please select a few of them.

Those who know of a deadline looming know that a new lifeline extends, and that life can be extended through a firm footing.

Like steps of a pyramid, one step's end becomes another step's commencement; the stories of life pass us over or become the foothold for new ropes of attainment.

I sift through the myriad of sands. I search for those grains that rub both reader and leader raw against a skin of complacency. I trust that this will expose the scrapes of truth, the blood of reality, the flesh of substance, the tendons of snapping grace, the bones of broken beauty, and the blood of elegance—revealing truth in a manner that I can no longer ignore.

Oh, how we do hate to get beneath the protective covering of it all, so we take the necessary covenants to rip off the scab again and again.

For in so doing, I expose the clothed reality of scandal, pain, hurt, and deception, and get to the truth you shine upon me.

I heal and reconcile, and I become grateful for those places and experiences that ultimately result in thanksgiving.

Le Cou

There is that place above the collar of your shirt, at your nape and just below your hairline, that my lips long so desperately to touch.

The shock and ooh ... of such warm and slightly salty flesh makes my mouth salivate and my crotch heave a heavy sigh in fatigue of strain.

Could that fabric against your neck be lowered, removed, or cut away?

To remove my imagination to a reality in flesh and provide me more acreage to romp and explore such simple pleasures as my own hot breath?

Bearing down on the shores of your neck flesh.

Just that one area is all that it would take for my mouth to feel satiety and for your body to be consumed with a pleasure that is great.

May I cause the length of your back to disengage from the surface and feel as if your spine would snap?

What powerful pleasures await the fire from within as I rasp against your neck with my razor-smooth chin?

Now suck in one last breath of scale and scope from this episode quixotic, and know that was just the beginning of a thought, a moment, and a hope to be spent

Alone in alone and love upon love.

Lamentation

There is a place down a long and winding corridor that leads to an open area. There is no door to it, and only I know how to get there. It is where I go most often when I want to feel the full expression of my despair.

The warmth of deep sorrow comforts me like the sun in a grassy meadow. How it does engulf me and warm my skin. The heartache of opportunity that exists within my chamber causes me to close my eyes and bask in the sweet solitude of the disenchantment within my innermost being.

To rest, to be still, to allow my mind the freedom to delve the depths of my regrets and self-induced shame and know that all beings, especially those who have known and experienced greatness, have all been visitors to their own experience of this expression.

And, yes, I felt great self-compassion and great understanding through remaining in this place alone and undaunted. For from this place can a great person retreat and know firsthand his or her once-humble beginnings.

Allow the bellwether of personal knowledge to guide you back to your position of honor, and know that this is a place for your comfort and strengthening.

Those who dare to brave the journey again for the knowledge of existence can endeavor to fill the hole that never completely goes away. It remains as a constant and gentle reminder to those who know and understand how necessary it is to heed the call of the place of trust.

That place is their very own gut.

Visitation

A wealthy man, who happened to be a New Yorker, came home one day from the florist shop to make preparations for a dinner party in his home. In his arms he carried a bunch of white chrysanthemums, a bunch of long-stemmed white roses, and a single lily, which he would arrange in his home to greet his guests as part of the evening's preparations.

He realized shortly after his arrival at his home on the Upper East Side that he had forgotten a few things, so he went back out to his local grocer to get the things he needed. While he was gone, the flowers began to talk among themselves.

"Hey, Roses, why do you think our owner only bought one lily?" asked Chrysanthemums.

"I am not at all certain," said Roses. "However, I am sure it is not from lack of money."

Chrysanthemums and Roses talked among themselves for several more minutes, completely ignoring Lily. They talked about her and around her, but never directly to her.

This seemed to faze Lily not one bit. She simply rested on the kitchen counter next to Chrysanthemums and Roses, in a state of quiet repose.

When the man returned, he selected three vessels worthy of each flower type and prepared their new homes for placement. In each vessel, he put fresh water and chose various flat altars of distinction to place each arrangement upon.

Chrysanthemums' altar of distinction was a circular Regency table in the main entryway of the home. She was simply elated that her full blossoms of glory would be on display for the owner's guests to see as soon as they walked through the front door. *A fitting place for me indeed,* she thought to herself and let out a shriek of giddy floral laughter as her owner placed her upon the table.

Roses' altar of distinction was the living room table. An exquisite masterpiece of glass and polished steel would serve as the foundation and support for an array of beautifully fragrant and elegant roses. When the owner set the vessel down on the coffee table, the sun and the skyline illuminated their radiance upon Roses, and she was exuberant with pride and joy as her essence filled the room.

When the time came for Lily to be arranged, the owner simply placed her in a plain cylindrical glass tube that was one-quarter filled with water, and then he set her on the dining room table.

Chrysanthemums and Roses both looked at Lily and burst into laughter, for they knew that a dinner table was the kiss of death when it came to flower placement. Overshadowed by the food and ignored by the guests and their conversations, poor Lily would be utterly and hopelessly forgotten throughout the entire evening.

Lily neither acknowledged her plight nor uttered a word of dissent. She simply remained silent and accepted her place of resting, regardless of how disrespectful her assignment seemed in that moment.

At the appointed hour, the guests arrived, and as if on cue, each and every person entering the home gushed and lavished praised on the beauty of the Chrysanthemums, commenting on her place of honor and her exquisite features. This praise only caused her to arch her stems upward ever more, pushing fragrant beauty out into the air with radiant glory.

As guests wove their way through the man's home, talking, chatting, and enjoying appetizers, they eventually began to fill the living room, where, once again, praise and astonishment were lavished upon Roses in all of her aromatic beauty. By this time, Roses, with her petals splayed wide open, basked in the waning rays of the sunset, which served to be synchronized with the drifting compliments of her well-heeled admirers in the room.

As the evening progressed, food was served, conversations were developed, and, yes, Lily was ignored. Guests dined, drank, and left. Food was placed in containers, and the home was cleaned up.

Silence fell upon the man's residence late into the night.

The next day, he woke up, brewed coffee, and checked his messages.

There was one message:

> Hello. This is Marilyn. I am sorry I could not be there yesterday. The pain of my son's death was still fresh in my heart, and it is still too soon for me to be engaged in social engagements at this time. Barbara and Larry called me when they got home and told me that the party was fantastic. I would have expected nothing less. They also mentioned that, strangely enough, your dinner table had only one lily on it, which was very uncharacteristic of you, someone who loves flowers … lots of them.
>
> I have to tell you that hearing that you had a single lily on the dining room table sent hot, salty tears down my cheeks, as it was the most beautiful thing I have ever heard of. I was deeply touched that you remembered my son was carrying a white lily in his hand to bring to me before he was shot in the heart by a stray bullet in Central Park. It was as if you had placed my son at the dinner table to honor and remember him in the midst of your party. I am so grateful and will never forget that simple gesture of kindness you gave to me, even though I could not be at your home. I love you so very much. Good-bye for now.

The man released an audible sigh and gave a shudder of gratitude when he felt the presence of Marilyn's little boy with him in his home, as if to say at some unseen but heartfelt level, "I know what you did, and I am so happy that you blessed my mom in that particular way."

Right at that very moment, the man looked over at Lily and saw that she had surrendered her flower petals to the top of the table. He looked at the flower for what seemed an eternal second, and smiled.

Tight-Mouthed Life

Keep your damn mouth shut, man!

If you do nothing else from this passage, then heed this note:
If you desire long life with your wife, mate, or spouse,
men of all ages, races, types, and styles,
a closed lip will serve you like a beautiful smile.

Career, kids, and business headaches,
are these a match for you and your comparable life?
With today's modern woman, who indeed has it all,
don't let your mouth become your downfall.

For when power, wealth, and strength were the rule of the day,
a man and his might were all you needed to be okay.

So now, in our modern life, why has this all changed?
Because now women have what we had, and we now bear the pain.

Being the man and being thought of as the liar,
Because your flapping gums put your ass in the crossfire.

A set of flatulent lips causes a bent spatula to the neck,
as a result of your thinking you can keep her in check.

Do not let, time, education, or evolution cause you to think
that your words are effective; man, your words just plain stink.

What man can say he ended up in court
because he successfully kept all his words short?

Now how many men have used words with turbulent force
and saw their fortunes cut sharply while in divorce court?

You dumb and foolish man, who told you that you would rule the roost?
Did your ass feel this result from her hard steel-toed boot?

Go ahead and let her say you communicate without charm,
as your mouth, sealed like Fort Knox, will keep you from harm.

So now I leave this last phrase, and it's all up to you,
a quiet, detached man shall be your new pursuit.
And after the argument has passed like bad wind,
know that your clenched jaw did keep you from sin.

That you have done it and have mastered this art,
and know you can move forward with a lightness of heart.

And even if you're called a man of few words,
it's much better than being trapped like a blabbering caged bird.

For when you master your mouth and master the silence,
you will always avert harm, shame, and future violence.

I wish you much luck as you take this to plan,
and at long last become a quiet and most peaceful man.

Every Time

Every time and time again, I deliver you to me and don't receive.

Every time and time again, I am hammered and harangued without reprieve.

Every time and time again, there is a constant sliding of the door; and every time and time again, the warden of wife comes here no more.

Every time and time again, I am relegated to a place of disdain and tolerance.

Every time and time again, I am without remark for being a mute of beaten-down insolence.

Every time and time again, you do my psyche bodily harm; as every time and time again, I extend my hand and you sever my arm.

So now this time and never again shall you be my recompense.
Because every time and time again, I am free to sing and do my own dance.

Entwined in Rhythm

The sweet serenity of your gentle touch is like an intimate tango that transcends emotions.

The beautiful music your skin creates becomes curves of light that dance and illuminate my mind.

It is a delicious and delectable thing to have my very countenance so deeply rocked by another, and yet I know that this too shall come to pass.

The winding and intertwining of hearts, like strings, till our lives become an entangled and intractable mélange of knots and ties.

What pair of scissors can cut them all at once? For if one were cut, there would be a myriad of others to keep the connections.

A wonderful thought does come to mind.
My love for you is simply enough.

Melancholy

Melancholy of melancholies.

A feeling of desolation pervades this city street.
The lights of the buildings are bouncing off the backs of my eyeballs, and they beckon me to enter into a soft, sultry, sad existence within their hearts.

A hearth that contains fire and yet gives no warmth; what the fuck is that? What use can such waste of light and heat be for?

From the outside it seems so beautiful and warm, dreamy and Dickensian in its very presence.

Out on the street, where only God knows or can tell what might be for me, as I stand here shivering and cold.

I don't know why I have chosen to allow my heart to long for such an impossible thing, and I don't know why the great I Am has brought this misery into the neurons of my mind and capillaries of my heart.

Where are you when I need you most?
Have you developed amnesia and suddenly forget my name, my countenance, my presence, and my need for you?

I did abide, and you did not abide back in me. Was that just some simple prank to make a punk out of me?

Am I your concubine, to be summoned as you will and when you want? Do you seem displeased now that I have given myself over to you? Oh, what is the fate of a lost soul in this experience?

Can I now go back to where I was and hit the replay button? If only life worked so simply to rewind and re-create. And yet if I did that, would I be in an endless speculation loop?

Fuck it. I am going to go home, go to bed, and go to work tomorrow.

Coffee does make the world more bearable, and I can experience a moment of joy in its simple pleasure, if nothing else.

Frack

"You see, God took the taste for that out of my mouth, and I am so grateful," said a very dark-skinned, older gentleman as he shined my shoes.

We were on the second floor of one of those ubiquitous marble high-rises in downtown Dallas. I wanted to ask so many more questions of this man.

Why did he tell me about his salvation?
Why did he tell me he had a drug addiction?
Why did he talk to me as if he had known me all his life?
Why did I wear such hideous shoes that didn't even seem worth this man's time to be polishing in the first place?
What was it about our meeting that caused this man to speak to me as if I were his closest confidant when he barely even knew me?

I sat there and studied this man as he continued to talk to me; he kept talking for the entire time he shined my shoes. Initially, we spoke of the things that are commonly talked about when seeking to be polite, passing the time without being overly dramatic or political: where I was from, where he was from, people that he knew from my area, and the food that I loved from his area.

The conversation surprisingly moved in a technical direction when this man started talking about oil and gas exploration and the practice of fracking, which he seemed to know a great deal about. He shared with me that this practice was ruining the groundwater in Texas and that people now had to move from their land or buy land that was far away from where there would be fracking in the near future. What was particularly interesting to me was that the former oil executives who had grown wealthy from their careers in oil and gas were now the very same individuals buying up large tracts of land in order to protect and ensure that they and their families would have potable water for generations to come.

The man shining my shoes was as gentle and polite as you could imagine, and in a way that only a genteel southerner can express to another person. The undulating lilt of his voice would rock you to sleep if you allowed yourself to focus on the tone and pitch of his vocal cadence. And yet, at the same time, I would never wonder whether he was carrying a concealed weapon. It went without saying that he was. It wasn't a question of *if*; it was a question of *where*.

As I left, giving him a 40 percent tip on top of his shoe-shine service, I could only feel that I was the one blessed by meeting this man, and not the other way around. His presence shone more brightly than that of any movie star, and his gentle, soft-spoken presence was as disarming as that of a baby kitten.

It was just one of those days where I was grateful to live long enough to experience a moment of service, connection, and love.

Li'l One

Still, small voice inside me, why are you called "still"?

> I am called *still* because my words are easier to understand when your physical self is at rest.

Still, small voice inside me, why are you called "small"?

> I am called *small* because when I am tiny, your mind's eye draws down and into me with a ferocious intensity and focus.

Still, small voice inside me, why are you called "voice"?

> I am called *voice* because I have sound that speaks clearly to that part of you which already knows how to do what you need to do; you just need a gentle way to remember.

Awaken

Creativity is a process that can be opened at any time. Creativity loves a disciplined mind.

What discipline says to creativity is this: "You are so important to me that I am going to give you my greatest gratitude by showing up prepared for you!"

Creativity responds sure and true to your steps of faith by giving you inventions to patent, paintings to finish and sell, dances to perform and choreograph, books to write, discoveries to document, and songs to sing and scribe.

You see, creativity gives others permission to execute their vision and to be able to do the things which they thought were too silly.

There is an engineer waiting to learn about another engineer who quit her job to become an opera singer and thrive in her new career.

For the sake of their own security, there will always be those who create as a part of the vision of others. And those are the very same individuals who lie on their deathbeds wishing that they had taken more risks in their lives.

What serves your soul the most?
The opportunity of tomorrow fulfilled by what you are doing right now.

Place of Rest

The mind is like a garden of infinite nourishment.
I retreat to the green forest which resides in a space behind my forehead.

The warm beaches of the Mediterranean reside at my inner right ear.
As for the desert, when needed to warm my wounded spirit, I quickly go to the base of my neck.

What my left inner ear gives me is like having a virtual library in the heavens.
It is a place that serves as a resource, allowing me to change and grow according to my need.

And I say they all coexist, or do not exist at all, based on what my soul needs.

Sometimes my soul needs to find peace.
Sometimes my soul desires to keep peace.
Sometimes my soul longs to regain peace.

They are 100 percent effective and require no extra luggage, for they are always with me, safe and sound. They give me great comfort in a world that seeks to steal them from me at any moment.

I guard them as if my life depends on them, for my life does indeed depend on them. These spaces and places nurture me, strengthen me, and treat me kindly. It is what I always get from them when the world lets me down.

When I am let down, I find a place to rest.
When my heart is broken, I find a place to rest.
When I am wronged, I find a place to rest.

Thanks to these places and thanks to these spaces for keeping me sane.

When life lets me down ... to find peace ... I stay strong.
When love breaks my heart ... to keep peace ... I grow whole.
When I am wronged by others ... to regain peace ... I heal daily.

Battlefield of My Mind

Between the realm of space
and the realm of time,
rests the battlefield of my mind.

The place I know
I have seen before;
it's a busted up field
pockmarked from war.

A war that rages,
a war that's wagered,
every morning, noon, and night.

Oh God, what is it
that I must do
to stop this unending fight?

When time brings challenge
and a fragile imbalance
does not yet bring a new thing.

It's when space meets fate,
God does participate
to bring forth
a salve to life's daily sting.

He feeds my soul
and my wallet; it knows
who made this happen
and to whose kindness
I fasten.

I receive the blessing
that comes with his giving,
and I know this is
a hundred percent true.

That the field does heal,
and with every new deal
my world does increase,
and my worry is ceased.

His love provides,
so my faith does not relent.
I do know now
that I can make a U-turn from old thinking.

In this space
and place,
I make a new field
that is a place of creation.

Can you imagine a nation
if we all learned and exacted
this truth
as our passion?

We could and would
change the world,
and the angels constantly herald a God that is great
and who suspends us in faith.

Now go, and doubt no more;
and cause this knowledge
to open doors, and do not be let down.
Seize your rightful crown.

What is it that negative people
and people of poor moral character
and some who are wealthy, who know what is right,
do wrong and do harm?

They may get richer quicker,
and yet the deathbed does not give a damn,
for all bodies are equal
when the grim reaper comes for payment.

Is this the wrong question to ask?
I should ask, how is it that my dreams come true?
And I get more money, success, and good fortune,
No matter what I do.

The Creator hopes and prays that all good changes hearts
for the benefit of others,
our sisters,
our brothers.

And I do not know the hour
when a despot will perish,
or learn to cherish that which has been given
for the good of others.

Eventually, it will all go to good hands,
to heal hearts,
to heal minds,
to heal the land in the service of kindness toward others.

It binds the whole together,
whether you know this now or later.

A new beginning,
every single time.
That is the end
of this line.

Outcome

Life has an amazing quality in that what I gain in my tomorrow is as a result of my present and is not dependent on my past.

Consequences do endure, and they can unsettle and cloud the path that I should take.

Consequences are not a life sentence or a call to action; they are merely an observance of what has been done to affect what I am currently doing.

A novel can just as easily be written from a penthouse desk as from a jailhouse cell.

And yet the impact can be profound for an individual, according to his or her desire to be heard, to be represented, and to be known.

Stretch and Withstand

As I bend,
As I stretch,
Stretch my soul,
Stretch my mind,
Mind gets soft,
Mind grows stronger,
Stronger in spirit,
Stronger in ability.
Ability gives opportunity,
Ability builds confidence,
Confidence brings decisions,
Confidence tempers ego.
Ego can control,
Ego gets subdued,
Subdued into remission,
Subdued by love.
Love helps others,
Loves gives hope.
Hope can help,
Hope can heal,
Heal my heart,
Heal others' wounds,
Wounds left untreated,
Wounds left abandoned;
Abandoned in despair,
Abandoned through surrendering;
Surrendering to stupidity,
Surrendering to others;
Others' fueling fears,
Others' sheer lack;

Lack of greatness,
Lack of knowing;
Knowing with God,
Knowing with faith.
Faith creates space,
Faith brings power;
Power to know,
Power to change;
Change a circumstance,
Change a fate.
Fate does follow,
Fate must conform;
Conform to vision,
Conform to destiny.
Destiny is inevitable,
Destiny can withstand;
Withstand the fight,
Withstand the fear,
Fear from others;
Fight to succeed.

Small Miracles

I sit and watch the rain cascade down my window,
and lament at the loss of my wife.
As I do this, a sparrow comes to rest on the railing of my balcony,
and looks out over the horizon of my yard.
A slow, hot, salty tear drops from the lower lid of my eye,
and at that moment, I feel the warmth of the sun on my face.

Every small thing is a reminder of my blessedness.

What happened to my heart that I should forget what has brought me so much joy?
And whom shall I blame for this lapse in judgment?
The pain of my self-scrutiny is too much to bear,
as I know the blame serves as a boomerang every time.
And when I leave this earth, what will I say to her
as we meet on heaven's doorstep in a lifetime of eternity?
I shall not be disappointed with that thought.

Every small thing is a reminder of my blessedness.

My father's father did teach me well:
Work hard, work steady, and enjoy what falls from the tree;
eat what has been given to me.
And as I complete that thought, my wife comes through the door.
She smiles and is radiant.
And I remember that we are still here.

Every small thing is a reminder of my blessedness.

Twenty Inspired Souls

1. Maya Angelou, for your velvety words of comfort;
2. Ken, for showing me the light;.
3. Richard Branson, for your Viking strength of purpose;
4. Austen, for your gentle strength and wisdom;
5. Barbara King, for your expansive love that envelops;
6. Michelle Tong, for your smile and joyful spirit;
7. Myron King, for being a nonstop, fierce faith fighter;
8. Matthew SMGST USAF, for being an anchor in the storm;
9. Sophia Loren, for no one is more beautiful of heart than you;
10. Sylvia, for thirty years of inspiring the dance;
11. L. Lambrou, for teaching me how to forgive;
12. Chris Hannon, for being a patron to my soul;
13. Yolanda Jordan, for telling me, "You can do it!";
14. Mark King, for rising above it all;
15. Brian Howden, for motivating me to say, "Yes, I did it!";
16. Suzanne and Sally, for transplanting academic excellence in me;
17. David Kopay, for showing me another way;
18. Peter Yao, for crowning the king in me;
19. Kathy, for your tenacity, which is like a rabid dog in a henhouse;
20. Karen Joyce, for being the powdered sugar that makes every dessert taste better.

Helpless Hand

It is a grievous thing for persons employed in service to others to be in a focused effort to achieve the objectives of their clients.

And to have advised the clients in thoughts, words, and deeds, and then to know that the clients have chosen to take their own counsel and take action to their own detriment.

The grievous thing about this comes not from knowing that those persons employed in service to others were right in their advice.

No. It comes from knowing that at the moment of the final decision, the clients chose unwisely and therefore must get the full and irreconcilable consequences of their choices after the harm has been released into consciousness.

Take wisdom in the experience, Mr. or Ms. Service Provider, and improve upon your activities when choosing your words with future clients.

And know that your grief shall be compensated by the fifteen-fold glad tidings of those who choose to heed your wisdom.

Take no solace in vindication, for there is no victory to witnessing the self-inflicted wounds of your service recipients.

Can a mother retroactively prevent her child's split lip or bruised knee or a gift stolen from him or her? The tears still come, and the inconsolable cries unfurl, and all she can do is wait and expect.

Expect that those experiences, when thusly repeated, shall have less hurt, less impact, and, hopefully, less chance of reoccurring.

Fountain of Proof

Passion is like an artesian well. When the pressure below the surface becomes too weak to contain the flow of water, the water can't help but seek the path of least resistance, and thus it gains access to the light, air, sun, and atmosphere. Once there has been a breach in the containment of the well, the water molecules seek to get out to where they have the opportunity to be a source of nourishment to the earth, trees, plants, and environment, all for the edification of others.

The Power of Words

If Satan were an object, what form would he take?

He would take the form of a razor-sharp tongue in the mouth of your spouse.

He would take the form of a razor-sharp tongue in the mouth of your boss.

He would take the form of a razor-sharp tongue in the mouth of your friend.

He would take the form of a razor-sharp tongue in the mouths of your kids.

Is there no better weapon for the quick and efficient destruction of an uplifted soul?

Praiseworthy Praise Worthless

I shall never utter the words "praise the Lord" again.

I have cussed out my wife.
Praise the Lord!

I have slapped the shit out of my child.
Praise the Lord!

I have cheated on my spouse.
Praise the Lord!

I have lied to my coworkers.
Praise the Lord!

I have rage in my heart.
Praise the Lord!

I have taken the life of another.
Praise the Lord!

I have stolen from my relatives.
Praise the Lord!

I have done wretched things in my life.
Praise the Lord!

I would sell my soul to get ahead in life.
Praise the Lord!

Instead, I will choose to let my life choices praise God daily. That is enough for me.

I took out the trash the first time I was asked.
That is enough.

I fed a beggar man.
That is enough.

I withheld strong judgment of another's circumstance.
That is enough.

I picked up after myself.
That is enough.

I thanked my colleague for her help.
That is enough.

I live with integrity toward all.
That is enough.

Six

Today, am I simple?
Today, am I whole?
Today, do I forgive the lies I was told?

Today, am I freed?
Today, do I smile?
Today, what does matter is what is worthwhile.

Homer

Set your sights high when engaging in a new business or art form that is begun with passion.

Cast your net wide when considering the recipients who shall be blessed by your undertaking.

The speed with which your idea excels is based on the quality of the ingredients and the science of their combination in mass.

The stickiness of that combination of elements shall be the tangible force that divides your brainchild into its individual components and acts as the potential then reactive force that propels your concept into its propulsive apogee.

Let love and companionship work together to make the long hours of trial and toil seem like play and fun.

Designate a single point of leadership to shepherd the vision and remove obstacles as they come.

Expect a quickening as the idea moves from conception to completion, and allow the law of success to do what it does best, which is to repeat itself again and again.

Hard Air

The most important thing about taking a leap and making contact with the ground is what happens in between.

Death is a leap, and regaining consciousness is the ground.

Anyone who has had this experience with remembrance can explain in vivid detail what he or she has experienced in that space of time.

All over the Map

Walk with me, then
ahead of me, for no particular purpose.

I can't keep up with you!
Retreat within my heart to a safer place.
Reject the retreat and acknowledge the disharmony.
I will not make up for lost time.

Go a different way to a similar outcome, and keep self-pace.
I will slow down.
I am on pace to achieve my dream.
I will stop and assess my situation, quickly.

I must remain here and take my mind forward.
I will start again in a slightly different direction.

Now resume your action based on the direction you set within your mind.
I will forge a path on the same plane; curve of action is now in synchronicity with intent.

Eventually, I rejoin you.
Come back to a place of common meaning.
I will keep pace.
Work to adjust your place based on your temporal assessment.

I will arrive with you.
Now regain your symbiotic rhythm with your recalibrated cadence.

I will rest content.

Changed State

How long will you endeavor to remain in your chrysalis state?
You see the transformation unfolding around you, and yet you stay

hidden,
protected,
unchanged,
unrelenting.

Do you not know that your beauty is given when you surrender?
Fight to stay, and a moth's decay eats at your sides as it would a well-worn sweater.
The threads chewed bare, and your circumstance has become that of a hole-infested beggar.

It is a state neither you nor I are designed to endure; it was for the changing and nothing more.

Will you please change?

And regarding your chrysalis, look to it no more.

Time to Grow

Hope came and set an appointment.
It showed up on time and full of energy.
Then Hope, as I was working with it, cut me at the knees and left me sidelined, confused, and deeply disappointed.

Then Opportunity, Hope's mother, knocked at my door. She was petulant and full of fire and ambition. Where Hope had gone I do not know; she lingered on like a weight that attached itself to an unseen, tangible reality.

I thanked Opportunity for coming to replace Hope.

Then, sometime later, Opportunity came again—larger, louder, and more brazen than before. She would not shut up and would not stop clamoring for recognition. So I partnered with Perseverance to manage the wild energy of Opportunity, and, together, we took Opportunity and fed her soul so that she could be released from her shackles and set free to grow.

Hope, where did you go?
You left me so suddenly and without explanation.
I have mourned you, asked you to come back and never leave me again.
You discard my pleas and do not respond at all to me.

I cannot let you go, so I will float you back to the surface from the depths of my despair. Give you light and oxygen, and resuscitate you more fully than before. For you didn't understand my purpose was greater than your rejection.

You may not look the same as before, and you will be even more expansive when you arise from your slumber. So now you are back, and I am here to pick you up and carry you to your new resting place in the sun.

Lotion for the Soul

A salve to the soul.
What does that word look like?
A balm to my hurts.

A welling up in the chest.
What does that sound like?
A quick moment to reframe.

A wind to uplift the blind.
What gentle breeze can do that?
A delicious aroma to breathe in.

Gratitude.

Horizon

Today is my last day on earth.
Earth from which I came is not where I must rest.
Tomorrow is not promised to me yet.
Yet I yearn to see the dawn over the mountains.
Yesterday shall be forgotten quickly.
Quickly I must resolve to find the one thing worth living for.
For my yesterday has left a faint impact on my today so that I might strive a bit longer till tomorrow.

Change Point

Temperature drops.
Ice crystals begin to form.
First one, then others from a small, humble beginning.

Others see that something unique is happening, and they conform to the process, not yet knowing what they are creating.
Eventually, all who are close enough and able to participate are eager to join the fold.

In so doing, they form frozen lakes that are used for transportation and enjoyment.
In so doing, they form blocks of ice to carve and sculpt.
In so doing, they create glaciers and sea ice that carve the land.

It's amazing what a simple, single, solitary ice shard can amount to over time.

Four by Twelve

Teamwork is the most destructive paradigm to the CreatorUnl.

Teamwork.
Destructive.
Paradigm.
Creator.

Singular.
Intensive.
Paradigm.
Idea.

Sequestered.
Cloistered.
Incarcerated.
Ensconced.

Agitated.
Restless.
Distracted.
Annoyed.

Argumentative.
Hostile.
Frustrated.
Inconsolable.

Exhausted.
Surrendered.
Resigned.
Exhaled.

Begin.
Awkward.
Progress.
Self-doubt.

Contriving.
Moving.
Accelerating.
Releasing.

Striving.
Protecting.
Expanding.
Nurturing.

Recreating.
Finishing.
Accomplishing.
Completing.

Serving.
Telling.
Sharing.
Growing.

Exalting.
Inviting.
Administering.
Delegating.

And so a life correction brings about a beautiful word selection.

Chris and Luke

Take a moment of time to reflect on your life;
recount what brought you here.
You with me, and me with you;
innumerable moments to renew.

What did you forge for eternity,
in hope and love?
And what is cheered and witnessed,
both below and above?

A consummate union,
two hearts are entwined like ropes of challah braided in delicious time.
A duo which dances, and a couple in flux.
A storm surge on certain days … those moments suck.

So much uphill climbing,
in a spirit that causes sweat and strengthens love,
which can seem at times unfettered;
and, yes, sometimes I do forget.

What was our last fight about?
Who cares? I will cash my paycheck.
The good, the bad, the more often forgotten,
the remembered, the cherished, and the indelible,
in friendship, as partners,
as one with one and also unique.

And when we are finished,
we know we have won the ability to say,
"You are mine,
and I am yours."
So let's lift up our glasses and cheer our lives—
you and me …
"Happy Anniversary!"

Momentary Retirement

After a long day of work,
Nothing is as comforting
As the familiar place of
Home
Alone—
No phone,
A soft blanket,
A comfortable chair,
A good book,
And, even better, a glass of wine.
Time stands silent,
And I am quiet.

Ruminations of a Successful Woman

Is it lonely at the top?

Often tired at the top, so that requires rest.
So I am alone when I rest, not lonely.

Is it lonely at the top?
Many try, few do.

What the top requires is to be here;
So it is elite, not lonely.

Is it lonely at the top?
I find that most do not understand the why behind what I do;
So I am shunned, not lonely.

Is it lonely at the top?
Most people fear being with me,
So I am forbidden from being with others,
Which is more sad than lonely, really.

Is it lonely at the top?
Others don't understand that I am here as a result of a process,
Not a position.
So the perception is based on a moment,
Rather than a single day of planning
Being repeated day after week after month after year after decade.

Is it lonely at the top?
I am never alone; I am with my best friend,
And my loved ones know who I am.
I am grateful for all this has brought me
And all that others have shared with me.

I am blessed.
It never occurred to me to think of my life in any other terms.

Is it lonely in the middle?

To the Moon

Purpose.
The fuel of the visionary's rocket
burns away, and yet its results stand firm;
goals are the vital lifeline that supports
what others call a deadline. A dead … line.

The creative influence of a visionary's idea
draws others to that vision, and it serves as a refuge.

It's like the shade of a mighty oak tree;
the cool, calming shade protects her recipients, and it is also a liquid nutrient
that supports the endeavors of the visionary.

Nourishment in Three Parts

Neurons of the mind
connect neurons of the heart
to feed the neurons of the soul.

Heal those soulful hearts;
concentrate no longer
on those who have harmed you.

And allow those who have helped you to
become the balm, the salve of your forgiveness.

Chlorophyll Fading

A dried leaf, paper thin in my hand,
once verdant and green;
a petite panel of nourishment
that supported an elegant maple.

When it was springtime in its life, it would recover
from being crumpled in my hand;
now in the autumn of existence,
it breaks into a million pieces.

I choose to have verdant young leaves in my hand,
and I will not crush the autumn leaf.

For I too shall be in the autumn of my life,
and I would cherish those who would share
a gentle hand on a parched and brittle body.

A New Hope

There was a man who planted a sunflower on the side of his garden shed, and it grew to be a beautiful, tall plant that the birds would flock to and feed from. He loved to see that sunflower work to grow and feed the birds. He called the place where he planted the sunflower "my spot of demarcation," because that was the spot that began his entire gardening career.

One day, a local garden vendor came by and told the man about some new plant seeds he had, and so the man bought a few from the vendor.

One of the seeds the man selected was a different variety of sunflower that the vendor promised would yield as much as, if not more than, any variety currently being grown. So the man planted the new sunflower next to his first seed, and he called the spot where he planted it "una nueva esperanza" ("a new hope").

The man watered the plants throughout the season, and they both yielded beautiful flowers and many seeds to feed the birds. Both plants were beautiful, each in its own way.

The next season, toward the end of summer, a little boy walking down the road with his mother saw the two sunflowers, and the man smiled at them and asked the boy what he thought about the two sunflowers. The boy asked the man why there were two different kinds of sunflowers, and the man explained to the boy how he had come to plant the two different kinds of sunflowers. He explained that the first one he found on his own and the second one was brought to him and he purchased it.

This was puzzling to the boy, and he said, "You found the first one; was there something wrong with it?"

The man explained that there was nothing wrong with it. He said that the first one was just a find and that he bought the second one because he was told it would be as good as or better than the first one. The man then asked the boy if he would like a seed from one of the plants.

The boy thought long and hard about it, and then he politely declined. The boy said, "You found your first plant. I believe that is how I should also get started. I found my first dog on the street, and he is always with me. There will be a day when he won't be my first dog, and no matter what, there is nothing like knowing that the first dog will always be the one where everything started. So I will have to find my own seed and plant it; otherwise, it would just be someone else's plant in my yard."

The man smiled and waved good-bye to the woman and the boy. He looked at his plants, smiled again, placed a rock by his first plant, and then went into the house.

The man died of a heart attack the next day.

The Clearing

The more I have come into my own sense of self and self-purpose, the more I realize how tired I have become of those who impede my journey.

The sooner I realize that those individuals are not needed for me to acknowledge my inner greatness, the greater my desire to see my life become a path to be followed rather than trodden upon.

The more I draw my focus inward, the greater my personal desire to increase my outcomes.

And the greater my personal outcomes, the more simply I can live in happiness.

Cartographer's Heart

The strings of the heart are real and tensile in their design.
They have been created that way and are fixed in number.
They carry pulses of feeling and emotion, much like a conveyor enclosed in a tube.
They also bring forth the purest form of feeling to their repositories, which rest at the end of each string.
These repositories send information, which is transmuted into vibration to the various areas of the body that each repository is connected to.

When words of anger hit the body through sound, velocity, and magnitude, they act as a switch that charges the heart and sends pulses of emotion from the heart through the heartstrings, and the repositories are flooded with these emotional pulses that completely fill them. Unable to maintain a static balance, the repositories open up their overflow valves and allow the volumes of what is known as toxic pulse waste to be flooded throughout the body.

The resulting physical and emotional manifestations are usually devastating to the self, and also to others, if they become the generating source for these magnitudes of toxic generations. If not dealt with immediately, these repositories lose their ability to naturally vacate themselves, and, therefore, they decrease in number over time. The net effect is this: the individual becomes incapable of responsibly processing any pulse that travels along the heartstrings, and then he or she becomes a toxic person.

There are many coping mechanisms that may be internally deployed, such as self-talk, and many external coping mechanisms that can be utilized, such as sex or painkillers. These are only temporary in nature and do not bring about the permanent restoration of the heart to its homeostatic state, which we commonly refer to as peace.

There is only one true and perfect remedy for stopping and reversing this damage, and that is the capsule known as forgiveness. The words *I forgive*, whether said internally through thought or coupled with an auditory expression, have the ability to instantly purge the entire system of all toxic material.

Each capsule is like clear glass and has streaks of red, like a marble, around its surface inside the capsule. These streaks are a potent gas that neutralizes the toxic pulse waste to be eliminated from the body, as slowly or as quickly as the person chooses.

The more ardently we give ourselves over to the expression of forgiveness, the quicker the elimination process. Billions of these capsules are released upon command, and their supply, like the universe itself, can never be fully known or exhausted by an individual.

This is the most powerful tool currently known to bring about the restoration of the heart—and it is called the heartstrings repository supply chain complex.

Tidal Joys

Waves of impact
reverberate on the seashore.
Your words are as such to me.

Capable of destroying an entire coastal city,
one phrase from you can be just as devastating.

The rocks of my heart, worn smooth over time,
as your gentle love caresses me and my heart's shoreline.

Be restored and whole, and express joy each day,
and your life will be as a wave capable of sweeping all doubts away.

Clean Sweep

2:15 p.m.

Val walked briskly to his office, grabbed his laptop off his green laminate desk, folded it up, and placed it in his black designer briefcase. He glanced outside for a moment, made some peripheral note to himself about the gray day on the other side of the windowpane of his office, and continued to proceed with a hurried departure.

Val noticed that he had left his day planner, an old-school business remnant he just could not seem to give up, and went back into the staff meeting to grab it, somehow a bit sorry he had left early to catch his flight to San Francisco. One last sweep through the office to say his good-byes and to make sure that he had not forgotten anything.

As he drove home, Val wondered what he would be walking into. Pushing the button on the automatic garage-door opener, he looked into the tidy garage, parked his car, and got out. The click of his boot heels on the asphalt and concrete signified that he was a man on a long mission, with a short amount of time to complete the myriad tasks necessary prior to his departure in fifteen minutes.

2:22 p.m.

Val went straight to work. He scarcely acknowledged his wife in the kitchen as he descended down the stairs of his home and immediately flung the dryer door open, pulled out a twisted pile of sheets, towels, socks, and underwear, and hurled them on top of the comforter and quilt piled up on the master bedroom floor from earlier this morning. The warm flannel sheets were always a tactile comfort to him; however, the leopard print pattern made it difficult to determine which was the lengthwise direction of the fitted sheet. Things like this frustrated Val momentarily, and he would quickly remind himself that he was just making the bed, not brokering the Middle East Peace Accord, and then he would immediately lighten up and focus on just getting the task done.

Fitted sheet, then the flat sheet, then tuck the foot of the flat sheet between the mattress and box spring, then tuck the corners in. Place the quilt on the bed; smooth it out. Place the comforter on the bed. Fold it into thirds at the foot of the bed so that it can be pulled up to the neck in one easy movement. Now the pillowcases needed to be put on. Shove the upper corner into the case. Pull the other corner into the other end of the pillowcase. Smooth out the case, and place each of the four pillows flat on the bed, so the top edges touch the headboard. Stack two pillows on each side of the bed. Make sure the flat down pillow ends up on his wife's side of the bed. Now place the five decorative pillows on the bed. Place three across the front edge of the down pillows and then two in front of the three pillows. Martha Stewart couldn't have made a tidier bedding ensemble in less time, even if her life depended on it.

2:30 p.m.

Towel folding. Val folded towels the way his mother folded towels. He had watched her do it as a kid, as a youngster, and as a teenager, thousands of times. He actually attributed his ability to wash, dry, fold, stack, and store linens and clothing in such an orderly fashion to her. Val smiled to himself, thinking about the time a good friend of his once called him to refold her bedroom sheets for her so that her linen closet would look as neat as when he'd folded the sheets she provided him when he was a guest in her home once. Val folded the large towels the same way every time, just like his mother did. Hand towels got the same treatment, as did washcloths. Val stopped just short of arranging towels by color, from light to dark, in the linen closet, realizing the futility of such measures would only cause him to develop an unhealthy obsession about the arrangement of areas of his home that only he would ever see. Obsessions were okay with Val as long as he didn't get too out of control with them. He didn't want to be like his brother, Vic, who actually measured the distance between the hangers in his closet. *Now* that *is obsessive,* Val thought as he finished up the towels.

2:37 p.m.

Vacuuming. Val took his Dyson Animal canister vacuum that was resting comatose and dismembered in the hallway and stitched it back together, plugged life back into it, and hit the red on/off button to begin the whir of the beater bar for the vacuum's journey across the floors. Quickly, methodically, and a bit forcefully, he ran the vacuum head over the cork flooring and wool carpeting. He felt an almost orgasmic satisfaction as he pushed and pulled the vacuum wand over any visible strand of dog hair, dead skin, dirt, or other intrusive object that marred his floors and rug. Val loved to vacuum, and he loved a somewhat orderly house. He didn't mind that the house looked lived in; it just needed to look like June Cleaver had cleaned house on a slightly off morning after pulling an all-nighter as a bartender back at the strip club. Val envisioned June as a double social agent who came home and beat her children frequently for mouthing off to her after a long night of fighting off overweight, philandering dirtbags. If swilling one too many gins and tonic before the white-bread husbands stumbled back into their cars to ride home to their pitifully perfect families was their lot in life, all the better. There had to be some element of back-door debauchery in those candy-coated perfect lives of the 1950s and '60s on television. Val shifted his thoughts to the task at hand and seemed satisfied with this vacuuming. Everything seemed to be in its rightful place … more or less.

2:43 p.m.

Porcelain-tile floor cleaning. Val came up to the main level to find his wife working a microfiber floor mop like a champ. Long quick passes across the floor, with just the right amount of moisture on the mop to remove paw prints and other stains, but without making the floor too wet for him to go over the surface with the beater bar. Val started at the garage door, worked his way down the hall and over the entryway wool carpet, and continued through to the kitchen. From there, it was on to the dining room and living room; one last pass under the desk, and the task was complete. At last, the house was presentable for the dog sitter, and he would not think that Val his wife were filthy hoarders now that they had given their home that look of "gently handled," rather than that of real people with too much work and too little time to put their shit away.

The futility of it all never lost its irony with Val. He always knew that he would leave the house and not give two shits about what the dog sitter really thought. He did it because his wife liked to leave a clean house, and whether or not there was time to actually accomplish the desired aesthetic was irrelevant. It would be accomplished. Period.

2:55 p.m.

Departure. Val and his wife got in the taxicab and made their way to the airport. Val loaded up his stuff and left the house … clean and ready for the dog sitter. He and his wife knocked it out of the park. The house was ready, and the two of them made it happen in record time. This was one for the record books: a clean sweep.

Specific Contractor

This is the dwelling that love built, from hands hewn from a heart of compassion.
The foundations built on a bed of hope so that the walls would sustain generations of loving-kindness.

Toward the homeless, the sick, the beleaguered, the downtrodden, the abused, and the forgotten. Those left behind and left for dead.

Who can know the potential existing within a broken heart that is extended a loving hand? Healing comes when your hand touches the wounded places, in love and earnestness and with honesty.

The house that is built on love shall never experience deterioration or decay, for it shall always be taken care of in the same measure as that which cared for others.
Let your home be a blessing to your heart, and let your family grow strong.

And know that a home whose walls are bathed in the rays of kindness shall endure all the days of your life, in the hearts of those you have served.

Return to Sender— Are You Kidding Me?

Success can be a disconcerting thing when it arrives on your threshold without fanfare. It merely shows up and delivers itself, as if to say, "What did you expect, another lackluster disappointment? Why are you so surprised to see me? Are you numb to my arrival? Did you not call my name to exhaustion? And yet, now that I have arrived, you do not recognize me. Once again, you underestimated yourself, but now you know. I am here for good and here to stay; so stop feeling so dejected, and get back to work."

Sleepy-Time Bus

Just let me go to bed;
rest, sleep, and forget
about the day today,
and what lies ahead … tomorrow.

And yet you beckon me to the one thing that I do not want to do.

Put my plan into action now;
you have goaded me into this.
I cannot stop until this task is complete;
the heart is not a respecter of time.
And my creativity knows not the meaning of nine to five.

So let me finish this task first,
and go to rest
with a complete heart and a vacated mind.

Jilted Winner

I will feel for you no longer;
you have led me down this path many times before.
I must change,
and then you don't;
I must learn to do things differently,
and I still see the same old, same old.
I can encourage or discourage you no more.
You have not yet come to the end of your rope,
the end of your hope.

Until you seek the discipline of another,
you are hopelessly fooling yourself;
and I play this game with you no longer.

Dreamscape

Do you ever
expect to dream
something that will
become your reality?

Why or why not?

Admiral and the Crew

Commander in chief;
yes, and thus granted,
by commander,
assistant commander,
and commander in training.

What can I do when I have not been called to a place of leadership to others
and for my own destiny's development?

Hide yourself from the rigors of social interaction,
and find a quiet place
to monk-ify yourself,
and remain there until
your inner vision
has completed your outward assignment.

Begin to see
that there are
only consequences
to challenge your inner peace,
and those challenges come
as opportunities
to strengthen
and bless yourself in the face of
your adversity and your destiny.

Royal "Oui"

We took it upon ourselves,
and then we understood;
we did not judge the messenger,
rather choosing the process
and discovering the result.

And when we did this,
we soon came to the knowledge that
messengers aren't perfect.
Indeed, their flaws are
interwoven between the math, logic, and phrases.

And in discovering the truth
behind intention,
we were grateful to be
what and where we are.

Requesting and being granted forgiveness, we went to work.

Halftime

If I had spent half as much time planning for my success as I did worrying about my failures, I would have been a rich man in ten years.

If I had spent half as much time looking at my own faults, rather than dwelling on the wrongs perpetrated against me, I would have been a healthier person in those ten years.

And the Creator Answered ...

"Hear me now, O people of great and patient suffering. Know that your call to me for restitution of what has been wrongly said about you and undeservedly acted upon you shall be halted, redirected, and acquitted upon request.

"Your time of gestation is now finished, and your full recompense shall be delivered unto you. Your precious hearts and your subtle resolve shall be lifted up to enable you to be the diplomats to your oppressors, and you shall be impactful around the world."

In a Small Package Is Greatness

The silence of your soliloquy shall overturn governments
and cause militants to have compassion for those they oppress.

Your integrity brings repentance to those who ponder the wrongs they have done toward others.

So lift up your fierce defenders, and protect your integrity, which squelches accusations.

As you bring about victory in wars both seen and unseen, know that you cause your detractors to surrender to you in humility and graciousness.

Fourteen Lines—
Are You Tracking?

Unshakable is my resolve,
unending is my joy,
unyielding is my passion;
forgiving is my surest response.

Believing is my first choice,
retrieving my purpose is my goal,
relying on personal inspiration
shall be the compass guiding my path;
I am therefore accomplishing a dream.

Remembering my childlike enthusiasm
descending from the lofty heights above in a form that I can begin
to condition my mind to focus
on the small parts first;
I will complete the whole as if by magic, and then it will be ready for all.

One Time ... Once More

I am certainly capable of remembering my greatest pains, sufferings, sorrows, and hurts, and from them, learning how to comfort those who have been brought to me for encouragement, allowing them to help themselves toward a better life of recovery and health.

Escape

How did I get here?
Hanging by a silk thread
and still believing my cocoon
will sustain my future
metamorphosis.

How did I come to believe
that this precious tensile existence
would continue to be a place worth living?

What is so stinking good about carving out a wedge of mediocrity within a pie that was designed to be a delicious and intoxicating celebration of all that is good, worthy, holy, and honorable?

Who benefits from my fear, which keeps me from moving in any direction?

*L*ovesick

Make no mistake,
we are at war
with systems designed by others to rob people;
those who would rather lie and cheat than give an honest day's work,
and lovers who do not love us back.

These are the things that cause us to grow, forgive, and move onward to reach those who cannot self-defend, self-protect, self-heal. In their own conscious and unconscious ways, they implore us battle-scarred warriors to be their solace and protection. In their time of great testing and trial, we do not bend, we do not fail, and we do not give in, because that is just what we do.

Attachment and Release

Know that you know that you know you are not alone. You are separated by distance, not time, from those who seek to truly know you as one of the fold.

Do you not know that you are the game changer, the reverse designer, literally throwing circumstances into reverse and yet moving forward?

A vehicle that has been on the wrong path for a long time will eventually collide without your screaming a word of warning to the driver, and the collision and carnage will most definitely happen if you don't scream. Your still, small voice is now a small voice still working to connect and correct the inexorable greed that was planted in a garden designed for many and then taken over by a few. It grows like a viral weed whose deed is to sow and never reap.

The recompense is its own strangulation, and now it looks to you for salvation from itself. And you have no other choice but to comply, to divide your tribe to do the necessary work and make whole what was once broken.

So Many Variables

What are we writing about today?

> I believe it is time to write about the space of trust in the presence of adversity.

The space of trust in the presence of adversity? What do you mean by "the space of trust"?

> The space of trust resides in a matrix. It has rules that govern it, just like the rules of plant life, photosynthesis, and new growth. Trust space cannot be redirected from the path that it must follow into reality. Much the same way that chess pieces can only move in a certain manner, so too does the matrix of trust have a game pattern in your life and the lives of others whose paths intersect with yours.
>
> If trust is destined to move forward in a linear path, or along a perpendicular trajectory, and then align with the heart's path, then an attempt to move trust along a diagonal path will always be met with resistance and interdiction. Trust has a way, a path, a direction, and its law of progress must be followed to be effective. In other words, you do not lead trust; trust is already established before you even begin to call upon her. You merely follow the path ordained to bring her from the realm of the absolute to the realm of the relative.
>
> You see trust as an esoteric, intangible thing or feeling, and yet trust is as real as an object on your desk or an article

in your home. She exists; she lives and resides always in the place between what is to be and what already is, and she waits in a state of homeostasis until she is called into being.

Trust can be intensified or decreased through your personal commitment to envision what has yet to be made into what already is.

The reservoirs of trust are greater than the oceans, and like a typhoon, trust circles from the elements around her and is drawn up like a great whirling funnel towering up into the sky. With enough power, nothing can escape her grip, and all who come to oppose her will be drawn up into her vortex, helpless to do anything except be a part of that which has been called into being.

So powerful is this word and action—*trust*—that great efforts have been made by men and women to encroach and squelch access to her reservoir, which is carried within each person. So to get her back—although she has never left you; it is you who abandoned her—you need only to stand still in that great reservoir, and let the laws of trust spring alive in your mind and imagination … and then watch the amazing gifts of trust come into being.

Recover

The road to failure is a beautiful path to endeavor to travel.
The smooth path to success has many paths of failure to accompany it.
Those who experience success without taking paths of failure become their own vehicles of downfall.

Choke Hold

Today, I breathe,
expect,
inhale,
and hope.

Give me the strength to
live,
give,
love,
and be foolish with my abundance toward others.

Give all,
give in,
strive not;
and weave effortlessly
with the threads of life.

Raveling themselves together,
from the molecular to the spectacular.

Cease your worry,
stop your hurry;
make advance preparation
to exceed your portion, and believe.

Breathe.

See Multiple Shades

Still, small voice, what would you tell me today?

> I would tell you that despair is the place where your mind goes when you have left your magnificent beliefs on the side of the road, thinking you were leaving them for dead.
>
> It's also the place where your mind goes when you look into the attic of your consciousness and realize that those dreams of yours, still sitting on their shelf, have become covered with dust and cobwebs. They have never gone away, for a dream can never be exterminated; it can only be acted upon, or not. The repository of that idea does not vanish, and its content never goes away. Dreams merely reside in your mind or in the world, and the choice is up to you.
>
> Your days have been assigned and numbered, and their increase or decrease depends upon your choices in health, wealth, and wisdom, so I would ask you to choose wisely and choose often.

Is that all?

> One last thing: love yourself with the passion that it would take to love every single person on this planet, and watch how your path goes from that of an ungroomed trail to that of a golden highway on which all things possible are transported from belief to reality.

Rut in My Gut

The road to reenchantment is a long one.
And yet, sooner or later, it is where I find myself.
So what do I do now that I am on it?
I could detour onto a side path and get off the road.
I could retrace my steps backward to the place where I first got on.
Retracing my steps is painful and oftentimes not more beneficial.
This current road ends in enchantment, although it does not seem so right now.
Stay focused on that, and keep walking.

E-Mythology

You can't be everything to everyone;
Can't be everything to everyone.
Be everything to everyone;
Everything to everyone.
To everyone;
Everyone.
Everyone can't,
Everyone can't be,
Everyone can't be everything,
Everyone can't be everything to you.

Right Number

When you seek me in your hour of need,
I can come to you with everlasting speed,
search the depths of your heart in your despair;
that's where you'll find me, the one who really cares.

When you were living large, with no cares for your soul,
and in your lust for now, you let your morals go;
it's when you're at your end that I surely show up,
knowing you took my love and kicked me to the curb.

That's when you needed me, and I did not forget
to come to your rescue, because I wanted to.
I will not judge your choice;
I will exult your voice.

You have the strength in you;
I give you all my love,
to the point of death.

My heart continues to long for you, simply because you choose to call me.
I was always waiting for you.

Oh My ...

Let me place the full weight of my naked flesh against you whilst probing your mouth with my greedy, thirsty tongue. Kisses so sweet, yet they never add an ounce of weight to my waist. Can such a delicious pleasure have no consequences? Indeed, the consequences are that I fall more deeply in love with you than I was the moment before. Let me say yes, and yes again, to your love and everlasting caress. A sweet, gentle grip and an all-enveloping embrace in love, passion, and trust; do I dare allow this intoxication to transform my spirit, my soul, my choice?

SMV Number 3

A note from the still, small voice:

Today, I need to talk to you about the process of Discovery and why it is so important to the creative mind, the entrepreneurial spirit, and the vein of productive outcomes that business professionals wish to pursue on their life paths.

Discovery is like sucking in a quick and full breath after being startled. You are in the process of doing something, and all of a sudden, from out of nowhere, arrives an event that catches you off guard and literally takes your breath away. Sometimes you are angry at the perpetrator, sometimes you laugh, and sometimes you make a discovery. This is what I am talking about: you make a discovery, sparking a moment of pure clarity about that which you have been doing, and it either propels you toward an inevitable, desirable outcome, or it brings about a sudden correction in your process of doing, enabling you to do what you had been striving to do, but with more ease, more precision, more joy, more elegance than you had previously known. And it is from this moment of discover that I gain my most ardent enthusiasm for your journey.

That is the beauty of Process—it is not the time spent on task that makes it so worthwhile; it is the discoveries that come in the doing that bring about the true necessity to seek a matter out, for in so doing, you become enamored with the surprises that come along the way. You learn to expect them and grow from them. That is where the beauty of discovery rewards all who do not forsake her.

Do Not Disturb

> The emotion of sex contains the secret of creative ability.
> —*Napoleon Hill*
> Think and Grow Rich: The Complete Classic Text

Still, small voice, what is the secret that Napoleon speaks of, and why is this secret contained within the realm of sex?

Sex has the ability to bring together more powerful feelings commingled with intense pleasure than any other medium. Think about it—joy, pleasure, pain, love, passion, vigor, heat, sweat, craving for more, orgasm. All these things require no additional input except your willingness to join in with another individual in the shared process of mutual pleasure and enjoyment. We use this physical, spiritual, and emotional activity as a means to connect with one another, and we think little or not at all of its pure force for creativity. Indeed, the greatest creative gift that there is for man and woman is the creation of life. Everything and all things that we know in this world come from it. Someone created the life that poured the concrete of the sidewalk that you are walking on now. Someone created the life that wrote the book you are reading at this instant. Someone created the life that designed the clothes you are wearing. And someone created the environment for all things possible in this world to exist so that you may choose your own destiny. What more powerful method can you think of that is capable of creating more than seven billion individuals on the planet today?

This creative secret is no secret; it is just not utilized, except for converting a select few people in the world into useful output, decisions, products, services, power, and money. Your brain's child, so to speak, is as capable of breathing life into a circumstance as into a new human being. Strange that we give it so little attention in application form, considering the lives that it impacts through the transmutation of sex.

Again

You took it upon yourself when no one cared.
Indeed, those same ones who made fun of you
now regard your hard-earned success as luck
or being at the right place at the right time.

Your heart is young in this experience,
no matter what age this self-recompense comes to your doorstep.

And then you recover from feelings of betrayal,
not from others, but to yourself,
because that which you knew years, weeks, days, or a moment ago
no longer held value to you.
For the betrayal is against your comfort in homeostasis.

You thought that was what you wanted,
until your soul could no longer stay satiated
in your big comfy chair.

You dared take one small step—
to the gym,
to your desk,
to your boss,
to your spouse,
to your siblings,
to your best friend,
And said, "Enough is enough."

I must begin again, even if the previous failures were painful—
Then the future of not giving it one more shot is crippling to your innermost being.

He will not be quiet any longer.
She will not stop until you start.

So now you begin,
or begin again,
or begin again, *again*.

Detroit

You have forgotten your former glory
and made such feeble attempts
to preserve her in her time of duress.

Moving on to greener pastures,
she was neglected and left for useless,
taken away and bulldozed,
ransacked and reinvented
somewhere else;
anywhere else.

You thought you could run from her pitiful situation,
and yet she followed you wherever you went.
And the lines of separation could not be maintained,
for they were made by man and without spirit.
Spirit would never accept such terms,
And, eventually, spirit would prevail.
He always does; he prevails now.

Despite all you have done to break him.
Now look at what you've done—
you have cast your unwantoness around the world,
and what you would not fix,
on one else could either.
Even the president could not rescue you from yourself.

And you will not be repaired until you choose to repair from within;
no new building can repair an old, rotten heart.
Revive the heart, and everything else will come back to her former glory.

This is simple but not easy.
Yet you can do it, if you choose.

Mocked

I stood hand in hand with the devil,
and he laughed at her about my plight;
for the hand that held was a ransom without bail,
and the price would cost me my life.

The devil stood at the top of her stairs,
and stared and puffed out his breast.
Whilst her face was pale,
and her tears did not fail
as she watched with sorrow through the night.

For a fool cannot know
the power of his foe,
when he willingly throws his soul to the one
who was always with his true love,
and released from above;
he could then pursue his fate … good-bye.

Six Things

Stop,
Think,
Dream,
Fret,
Interrupt,
Fear.

These six words encapsulate a human condition whose forbidden fruit seek to steal rather than impart knowledge.

Stop is related counterintuitively to Fret, because the human tendency is to move forward in fretting about a situation as a way to control and remedy the problem, rather than stopping and listening quietly for the right solution that comes from tapping into the spirit, which is directly connected to God, the ultimate solution seeker and provider.

Think is what occurs as the mind ponders, sending light particles through the space of the mind, seeking to reach and achieve solutions. Think is the antagonist of Interruption. Interruption loves to be ever present and is a singular force attempting to short-circuit the wiring of Think.

If Think, a multifaceted and multidimensional force for progress, good, and change, existed without the attempts of interruption to goad and thwart it, then Innovation and Creativity could not come as effectively to Think; for the mind would not be as exercised to overcome doubt and develop stronger solutions as part of the process. So these two words are like two worlds that act interactively and somewhat dependently on the process at hand, and when the knowledge that Interruption can be subdued and manipulated is understood, then Interruption actually serves as a catapult, propelling Think into an overriding force to bring something new forward into its own place in the world.

Dream, why are you so quickly and easily followed by fear? Why does a person's ability to dream get steamrolled shortly thereafter by a gripping feeling of *Oh shit! Did I really just allow my mind, my body, and my imagination to have that thought?* What are the ramifications of being able to be excited on all levels about a dream, so much so that it becomes an all-consuming passion, and therefore an inevitability to plan, create, and place that idea out in the communal sphere of existence, where it can grow and thrive?

Dream asks, who, what, how; Fear simply asks why. Dream asks: Whom can I get to help me accomplish this? How can I find the resources I need to make this happen? What is my next step to get this to reality? Fear asks: Why do you need to do this? Why do you think you are capable of this? Why can't you just stay where you are?

Dream is the coconspirator of all success, and Fear is the noisemaker who seeks to keep you diverted from your goals, at whatever cost necessary.

Stop ... Think ... Dream.
Repeat.

Agent Orange

From the window above, I could see the man in the orange jacket below walking toward the seashore of this artistic coastal town.
I stood quietly, solemnly wondering if he would continue to walk into the sea.

I decided to stop looking at what he might do next; instead, I created my own story:

He continued to walk straight into the sea.
His body reacted no differently in the water than it did on land.
His breathing was no different, even when the water went over his head.
He could see as clearly in the water as he could on land.

Whatever he wanted to see was there or came directly to him.
The whales would come to his presence and wait majestically for him to walk by;
as if to say to this individual, "O great one, what will you show us today?"

He wanted nothing and needed nothing. His presence was graceful and all that was necessary to bring the attention of the entire underwater kingdom to his recognition.

After several minutes of walking, the man in the orange jacket simply turned around and walked back out of the sea, onto the shore, and back to the place from which he came.

I have no idea where he came from or where he went. He simply chose to make his presence known to me, and I was comforted to have witnessed his beginning—and to have created his story and finished his purpose on this page, at this point in my life.

He was there, if for nothing else, to dredge up these words from my mind so that they could be placed on this page and complete this task. He knew before I ever saw him that he would be written into existence and therefore into eternity. He came for nothing else except to allow me a moment of reflection and progression, as if to say, "Come on, buddy, you are almost there."

And almost there I am, and so proceeding solemnly, quietly, from almost there to arrived, which is what my work must be in these next days and moments.

Art History

Peace will come through poetry as prayer;

and through a sun-washed painting that was created to break the heart of the most aberrant despot;

and as a long, still note embedded within the aria of a mezzo-soprano who unwittingly causes a head of state to become so enamored with her performance that he forgets to sign a war pact against another country;

and even through the grace of a human swan at the Bolshoi, the Met, Covent Garden, or La Scala.

Art is humanity, and if we learn nothing more than this, we must know that art is the most powerful preventative measure against corruption, greed, and the downfall of leaders, war and destruction.

What might the life of Adolf Hitler have been if he were admitted into art school in Vienna? For art was his first love. He who was rejected as unfit then became unfit for humanity, as a response to his first love being crushed and left behind.

We must do all that is necessary and noble and gracious to help others to each pursue that first love.

Humanity depends on it, if we are to change this world.

Four More Years?

Benjamin Netanyahu.
Barack Hussein Obama.
Vladimir Putin.
Xi Jinping.

Israel.
The United States of America.
Russia.
China.

Peace is needed.
Peace is brokered.
Peace is desirable.
Peace is probable.

Strand the four of them on a desert island,
without provision,
until they can create peace
and mean it.

No outside communication,
no outside assistance;
die if they must,
if they fail in their mission.

Make them agree before they can leave,
make their agreement a blood covenant;
if any one of them reneges on their agreement,
death is not a good enough judgment for any of them.

Now there is a true reason for the penalty of death to be enforced
when a leader fails to keep the peace;
then their head is a great price to pay,
and humanity is the benefactor.

Kisses

A kiss from a familiar face is a great thing to experience.
I was not expecting such soft lips on the surface of my skin.
Thank goodness I remembered to wash my neck.

CALaMity

There is serenity within the wounds of a broken heart.
Peace resides where calamity abounds,
for if wounding and calamity did not exist,
then there would be nothing to anchor peace and serenity to their places in life.

Les Yeux

Have you ever noticed that when you look into the eyes of some individuals, you simply see their pupils and the color of their eyes?

And have you noticed that at other times, when the same activity is performed, you can actually see into their eyes, as if the pupils and colors had a three-dimensional quality to them?

Have you noticed what happens to your heart when this second experience occurs? What do you think about when you recognize yourself holding your gaze or your gaze being captured for a period longer than just a casual glance?

There is a deeper, unspoken understanding going on at this level. A pair of eyes appears to connect and to wonder about what the possibilities are for the circumstances that led to this deep insight.

Haven't you ever wondered about the fact that when this deep connection occurs, it is as a result of your being invited to look beneath the surface of what appears to the visual senses, to what is truly appearing to the eye of the heart?

Revolving Door

Come into my life,
come out of my life,
come and go as you please.

I will not think of you when you are gone;
I will welcome your return, with a smile and a hug.

Do good deeds,
do great things,
do that which was not spoken.

And I will hear about your well-being
as the wind carries your news to my ears.

Love Control

What do we long for in our despair?
We long to be loved, and, more important, to know that someone loves us.
Uncontrollably.

We long for a day when that which held us captive becomes that which we are no longer captivated by, and in so recognizing "no longer," we understand that it is a process that takes time to win.
Uncontrollably.

You can't help but be won over by that which is greater than that which held me once captive.
Uncontrollably.

Steel-Toed Boots Required

I can love you as I love my own life, and my own life is not mine for the purpose of dispensing what I will, where I will, how I will.

The greatest tragedy of knowing one's own destiny is knowing that you allowed a person or a circumstance to suspend your destiny's journey.

Just kick the person's ass or that circumstance out of the way, and keep at it.

Illuminated Lover

A party of four sits at a table, in a beautiful restaurant overlooking the marina, and none of them talks to the others. They all focus on what is happening on their cell phones.

A woman sobs uncontrollably on a public transit bus because she has misplaced her phone and feels completely lost without it.

I am bereft, angered, and saddened when I don't find my phone immediately and have to take precious time from my day to find my phone.

Cell phone,
You are my solitary lover,
my companion in my time of need,
my 411, 911, one-on-one, the only one for me.

You make love to my ears with your constant ringing,
reminding me that I am important and needed;
that makes me feel like I am loved, which I am not.
I just pretend I am loved because I am needed.

When you are not with me, I feel lonely.
I get worried that I am missing out on something
if I leave you behind.

I will never forsake you,
and you are always there for me.

Sure, you sometimes get tired and drop my calls;
I always forgive you, don't I?

So, again, I thank you for loving me so much
and giving me everything I need;
my constant companion, and my pride and joy.

Red Dress

When life throws you a curveball, it expects you to catch it and play the game. On a Saturday evening in Anchorage, my wife and I walked into a group of motley-looking people, all wearing some form of red dress. Men and women alike in bad red dresses, bad red skirts, and bad red tops were coagulating on the street corner near Bernie's Bar downtown. I did not want to investigate further. My wife did; so we investigated further and found out this was a running group known as the Hash House Harriers.

They self-describe the ensemble as "a drinking group with a running problem." They come from all over the region, across the country, and around the world to a city near you, and this time that city is Anchorage. The purpose of their presence to run for charity. However, when we encountered them on the street, they were on their way to the Polar Bar. We said our good-byes, and then we got into our car to head home. My wife asked me if I wanted to go to the Polar Bar, and I said yes. So we turned our car around and headed toward the bar.

We picked up two red-clad stragglers who had gotten lost from their group, learning that all the group members have special names. Our two stragglers were known in Harrier circles as Mouthy Bitch and Betty Crocker. We got to the bar and engaged in various conversations while drinking beer. Two notable events were meeting a woman in a strappy red dress whose name was Pea Fart, and learning that we could get "sponsored" into the group by a guy named Puc. He was by far the most lucid person we talked to all night.

We were invited to join the group on a run the next day, told that Mouthy Bitch and Betty Crocker could be our sponsors. We thanked Puc for the invite, and my wife told me that she was ready to go if I was, which is our code for "Let's get the fuck out of here, 'cause these bitches are crazy." We went home and laughed a lot that night.

I joined the group the next day.

You Have Been Served

My heart has put a restraining order on my vocal cords,
and the court order to reverse the decision has been revoked.

Why should I allow this decree to be lifted?
And what more can be said that will make it easier to be understood?

My body and mind rails at the sequestration of my freedom of speech,
and yet the gag order will not be taken away.

So desperate is my yearning to speak out,
as if my voice can be the key to unlock the jail of my expressions.

Yet I know that he is right in the long run,
and I know that it is for my own good to be as such.

There is a great mystery in the unspoken,
and as my peace of mind is reinstated, I remember what it was like before
I was incarcerated.

The fighting inside ceases to be a problem,
and the agitation of my face melts away quietly.

Then again I do notice the peace that has again germinated,
and I reflect in silence on my solace once again.

It is then that the heart says, "speak";
and in the opportunity of that occasion, my voice remains mute.

The difference is, the freedom has been earned through suppression, and the suppression of bondage transmutes to suppression in freedom.

What a paradox when a desire to do that which cannot be made real becomes the desire not to do that which does manifest a new reality.

Crevices

I love to see the bare foot of a man who has worn his heel to the callused point of cracking and scaling.

The weight of his life and his responsibility have not crippled him. These pressures have given him a rough surface to press into and against, and his steps do not fail under the weight of the eyes and hands of those who depend on him.

His feet are firmly planted in his shoes and on the ground and in the world. He does not allow the tenderness of his youthful ways to cause his feet to become abraded or scored, like a knife that scores the flesh of a piece of meat.

The cracks and calluses he has earned along the way do him well and keep him from harm.

Alone and Loving It

If I am lucky, I wake up and find myself able to get up in the single-digit hours of the early morning and find peace.

My dog is still asleep and does not wake up from his doggie dreams. My wife is still in bed, and her peepers are still closed. I crawl out of bed slowly, slightly groggy, and go upstairs.

This is the most important and precious moment for me. It is that twilight time where I have no knowledge of what has gone on in the world, and I am alone. The entire house is quiet, and I can be at peace with myself in a moment of quiet repose.

The teakettle is not sputtering from being heated; the sound of my dog's jangling collar or his paws on the floor are nonexistent. There are no pots clanging, no words spoken; just the beauty of quiet, and no noise at all.

I can hear the blood flow through my body; I can hear the pulse of my heart through the inner canals of my ears. The blood flow actually creates a pulsing sound in my ears that I can feel and hear. So rare is that opportunity that I often forget that I have the ability to hear my body make its own music. It is the most precious earthly gift I know of, and its value is beyond monetary measure.

Order of the Genie

Nadir was sitting on the seashore, and he had his magic lamp with him. He wanted to speak to his genie, and so he rubbed the lamp, which summoned the genie up into his presence.

"Genie, I have a thought I would like to share with you. I know you are from eternity, and I would like to ask this question of you. If I were to have two books written about me, one book describing all that I accomplished in my life and another describing all that I have not accomplished in my life, which book do you believe would be longer?"

The genie responded thusly, "I have had some version of this question asked by many great masters through time, and I always respond with a story about one of the greatest masters I have ever had."

He paused and then told the story.

"One day, in the blazing sun, this great master of mine from the East sat down to an open book of two blank pages. The master wanted me to look back on his life and record two kinds of events. On the blank page on the left, he wanted me to record all the things he had endeavored to do and yet never accomplished, and on the page on the right, I was to record all the things he had set his mind to accomplish and actually did.

"My master then wanted me to predict whether he would be known as a man of forgotten self-promises, or as a man of great accomplishments who did those things which mattered greatly in his life and the lives of others.

"After some time had passed, I said to my master that whatever I wrote would not matter, and so I advised the master to leave the pages blank. I told him that if he still requested me to do this task, I would certainly complete it. The master then asked me to explain why I responded as I did, and I told him that the pages he wished me to write were merely two versions of the same story. They go hand in hand with each other, and they are the sum total of all things were worthy of investigation in his life. Some of the things investigated were also worthy of implementation. Everything implemented was a result of every other thing that was investigated and found not to be the most worthy use of his time in that moment.

"And then my master understood that he did not need to judge the faults and merits of his decisions; he needed only to be grateful that he lived one more day to exist and give merit to what his next choice would be.

"Those pages were never written, and he was a great master to me. Those who knew him carried his memory with them in their hearts."

Nadir thanked the wise genie, and then he observed the ocean in all its vastness and thought about how remarkable it was to be in such a beautiful place at this point in his life.

Clear Thought in a Moment of Hope

I do regret one thing in my life, and that is that if and when I have the chance to do something that brings me joy, happiness, and/or contentment, no matter how great or small, and I do not do that thing as a result of what someone else might think of me, then I will have lost out on an eternal moment to shine like the moon and give light to the being I was truly meant to express at that moment in time.

The Protector

Fiercely fight for the freedom to be your own individual, and emphatically resist all attempts to have your time stolen for the sake of a good cause.

Find a way to feed your soul as much as you can, until it is plump like a tick, filled with the blood of opportunity. And take care not to let your filled-up soul get crushed, with all the blood of opportunity exploding in chaotic fashion, without regard for where it goes.

Your creative ingenuity is a valuable gift that does not have time to be wasted on what you "should" be doing. Whatever you are doing, no matter how strange it may seem at the time, is bringing about a connection with people, space, place, and time that could not have been forged with the mightiest of hands.

That is why your destiny establishment is important, and the path to get there is made known from deciding to have an establishment.

God knows what the result will be, and sometimes an adventure is the map that is placed before you to help you gain the new skills necessary to bring your destiny into its existing place in the world.

Your friends and family will feel betrayed and dismayed by your bold actions and will scold and berate you for your wild and eccentric behavior. Remember that, when on their deathbeds, people do not mull over the mundane in their lives. Instead, they think about the opportunities that they could have taken but did not, to give more, to love more, and to be better people in all aspects of their lives.

You have the power right now to do something stupendous, and here is your personal invitation to go and find it now, to start working on what pleases you most and brings you the most joy in your life. And know that in pursuing joy you give and spread joy, for it is impossible to seek happiness and yet let it remain bundled up in a canister, never let out for others to see.

Peace.

Carrying Costs

Cottonwood seeds,
drifting everywhere,
causing allergies to flare,
and blanketing the city.

Pooling around the edges of puddles,
they proliferate for a mere few days;
their outcome mostly to never grow
or find place to root and take hold.

The few that do make it to fertile ground
take root and sprout,
and then many are torn out by the root to die an early death;
even fewer are cut at the stump, never to reach their full height,
and only a select few take root, grow tall, build strength, and weather the storms.

A proliferation of new cotton fluff will be their reward,
passing on the code of their ancestors
to a generation that will exist in a new environmental condition—
a condition that might be warmer than that of their fathers
or possibly colder than that of their mothers.

And, at last, they have their chance to determine if they have chosen wisely,
to be in the ground that gives them a chance to grow,
in the air that gives them a chance for respiration,
and under the sun that makes their opportunity shine—
to be that full-height wonder that brings about the cottony snow in summer.

Sleeping Cranes

A city slumbers under a cool blue sky;
no sounds of work are within earshot.
Cranes have not been flying;
the birds have not come again this year—
they were chased away, without regard for the future.

Now a city slumbers in quiet repose;
the remnant was glorious, and today no one knows
why choices were made and decisions unfurled
that brought on demise, and a town was hurled
into a malaise it can no longer not cure,
because the disease is no longer treatable.

The cranes never came, and they were never fed;
so now we are left as a remnant, forgotten;
a town that never became a city
that chased away the great birds in the sky—

to places that drew them with visions of light,
of sound and of hope,
to feed their own people;
and we here right now, hungry and broken.

I Have Found My Way Home

At last,
I am done.
I am finished;
I have completed the work.

That I was commanded to do from within my heart;
My still, small voice has made his debut,
And now he can rest and be quiet this day.

Knowing that all he wanted to express about these things
Has been done in a patient and diligent fashion.

At last,
I am done.
I am finished;
I have completed the work.

You have given me what I needed today, yesterday, and still tomorrow—
And at last.

Peace comes to me
And resides all around me; I am grateful and fearless.

What Is Your Poem and Story to Tell?

CPSIA information can be obtained
at www.ICGtesting.com
Printed in the USA
LVOW10s0617180717
541720LV00001B/237/P

9 781491 797846